Other books by
B. J. Gallagher Hateley

■ ■ ■

Telling Your Story, Exploring Your Faith

A Peacock in the Land of Penguins
(with Warren H. Schmidt)

Pigeonholed in the Land of Penguins
(with Warren H. Schmidt)

Customer at the Crossroads
(with Eric Harvey)

Is It Always Right to Be Right?
(with Warren H. Schmidt)

What Would Buddha Do at Work?
(with Franz Metcalf)

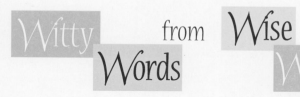

Quips, Quotes, and Comebacks

∎ ∎ ∎

by B. J. Gallagher

GIFT BOOKS
from Hallmark

BOK 5055

Andrews McMeel
Publishing

For all the wise, witty women
in my family:

■ ■ ■

my wonderful mother, Gloria,
along with Karen, Marilyn,
Auntie El, Doris,
Kathy, and little Amy.

Contents

■ ■ ■

Foreword

■ ■ ■

This little book is like chocolate. Chocolate delights,
energizes, comforts, and induces a wonderful sense of
well-being. You will experience all these feelings and more
as you indulge yourself in the pleasure of these pages. This
delightful collection of quips, quotes, and snappy come-
backs from wise, witty women will remind you of some of
your own experiences and thoughts about life. As you
savor them you will notice that, like chocolate, women's
thoughts and feelings come in different flavors—dark and
bitter, milky and smooth, light and creamy, and my own
personal favorite, the paradoxical bittersweet. Whatever
your preference, you'll savor these morsels of wit and
wisdom as chocolate for your heart and soul.

Arielle Ford, author of
Hot Chocolate for the Soul

BETWEEN US GIRLS

Wickedly Wonderful Women's Wit

■ ■ ■

Women say the darndest things! Women are smart; women are insightful; women are introspective; women are observant; women are sensitive; and, often, women are very funny.

"If I didn't laugh, I'd cry," we sometimes say. We laugh at the crazy predicaments we get ourselves into, and the crazy people in our lives, especially our families. Humor is one of our most valuable assets in life, helping us get through difficult situations without killing ourselves . . . *or anyone else.*

The ability to laugh at ourselves is the best kind of humor. It helps us see things in the proper perspective, and it keeps us from taking ourselves too seriously. As Elsa Maxwell encourages us: "Laugh at yourself first, before anyone else can."

Wit has truth in it; wisecracking is simply calisthenics with words.

—*Dorothy Parker*

I always wanted to be somebody, but I should have been more specific.

—*Lily Tomlin*

Deep down, I'm pretty superficial.

—*Ava Gardner*

The statistics on sanity are that one out of every four Americans is suffering from some form of mental illness. Think of your three best friends. If they are okay, then it's you.

—*Rita Mae Brown*

The telephone is a good way to talk to people without having to buy them a drink.

—*Fran Lebowitz*

I'm not offended by all the
dumb **BLONDE** jokes
because I know I'm not dumb . . .
and I *also* know
that I'm *not blonde*.

—Dolly Parton

The idea of strictly minding our own business is moldy rubbish. Who could be so selfish?
—*Myrtle Barker*

I don't have the time every day to put on makeup. I need that time to clean my rifle.
—*Henriette Mantel*

I refuse to think of them as chin hairs. I think of them as stray eyebrows.
—*Janette Barber*

You know the hardest thing about having cerebral palsy and being a woman? It's plucking your eyebrows. That's how I originally got pierced ears.
—*Geri Jewell*

A male gynecologist is like an auto mechanic who never owned a car.
—*Carrie Snow*

Who ever thought up the word *mammogram*?
Every time I hear it, I think I'm supposed to
put my breast in an envelope and mail it to
someone.

—*Jan King*

Can you imagine a world without men?
No crime and lots of happy, fat women.

—*Nicole Hollander*

We have women in the military, but they don't
put us in the front lines. They don't know if we
can fight, if we can kill. I think we can. All the
general has to do is walk over to the women and
say, "You see the enemy over there? They say you
look fat in those uniforms."

—*Elayne Boosler*

There are three ways to get something done:
Do it yourself, employ someone, or forbid your
children to do it.

—*Monta Crane*

Never lend your car to any to whom you have
given birth.

—*Erma Bombeck*

Always be nice to your children because they
are the ones who will choose your rest home.

—*Phyllis Diller*

A Freudian slip is when you say one thing but
mean your mother.

—*Anonymous*

Sometimes I worry about being a success in a
mediocre world.

—*Lily Tomlin*

Success didn't spoil me; I've always been insufferable.

> —*Fran Lebowitz*

I'm furious about Women's Liberationists. They keep getting up on soapboxes and proclaiming that women are brighter than men. That's true, but it should be kept very quiet or it ruins the whole racket.

> —*Anita Loos*

I'm extraordinarily patient provided I get my own way in the end.

> —*Margaret Thatcher*

When I was crossing into Gaza, I was asked at the check post whether I was carrying any weapons. I replied: "Oh yes, my prayer books."

> —*Mother Teresa of Calcutta*

Dear, **NEVER** forget
one little point:
It's **my** business.
You just **work** here.

—*Elizabeth Arden*
(in a note to her husband)

GIRLFRIENDS

Woman to Woman, Heart to Heart

■ ■ ■

A gay male friend once explained to me how he felt about men and women. "I *love* women," he said, "but I *lust* after men."

I thought about that for a minute and then replied, "Gee, so do I."

Men are great for sex (and a few other things), but I adore the women in my life. My girlfriends listen to me, give me advice, cheer my successes, console me in my failures, and even give me a kick in the butt when I need it.

My girlfriends are the strong, sturdy safety net I depend on as I fly on the trapeze of Life. They are flexible and resilient—they help me bounce back when I fall. Without them I would probably be dead, at least figuratively.

The men in my life may come and go, but my girlfriends are forever.

Laugh and the world laughs with you. Cry and you cry with your girlfriends.

—*Laurie Kuslansky*

Women best understand each other's language.

—*St. Teresa of Avila*

If we would build on a sure foundation in friendship, we must love friends for their sake rather than for our own.

—*Charlotte Brontë*

A friend is someone you can be alone with and have nothing to do and not be able to think of anything to say and be comfortable in the silence.

—*Sheryl Condie*

Plant a seed of
friendship;
reap a **bouquet** of
happiness.

—Lois L. Kaufman

Remember, the greatest gift is not found in a store nor under a tree, but in the hearts of true friends.

—*Cindy Lew*

I'm treating you as a friend, asking you to share my present minuses, in the hope that I can ask you to share my future pluses.

—*Katherine Mansfield*

Each friend represents a world in us, a world possibly not born until they arrive, and it is only by this meeting that a new world is born.

—*Anaïs Nin*

In a friend you find a second self.

—*Isabelle Norton*

One is taught by experience to put a premium on those few people who can appreciate you for what you are.

—*Gail Godwin*

It is not what you give your friend but what you are *willing* to give [her] that determines the quality of friendship.

—*Mary Dixon Thayer*

The only way not to break a friendship is not to drop it.

—*Julie Holz*

Do not save your loving speeches for your friends till they are dead. Do not write them on their tombstones; speak them rather now instead.

—*Anna Cummins*

Thank you, friend. I never came to you, my friend, and went away without some new enrichment of the heart; more faith and less of doubt, more courage in the days ahead. And often in great need coming to you, I went away comforted indeed. How can I find the shining word, the glowing phrase that tells all that your love has meant to me, all that your friendship spells? There is no word, no phrase for you on whom I so depend. All I can say to you is this, God bless you, precious friend.

—*Grace Noll Crowell*

MEN

Women Are from Venus, Men Are from... Pluto?

■ ■ ■

There are few topics that arouse such intense feelings among women as the topic of *men*. We have a love-hate relationship with the opposite sex.

We *love* their attention—it makes us feel appreciated and valued. We *hate* their attention—it makes us feel like sex objects.

We *appreciate* their male energy—it's intriguing, intense, and stimulating. We *deplore* their male energy—it's competitive, combative, and causes trouble.

We *admire* that male-bonding thing because it's tight and impenetrable. We *hate* that male-bonding thing because we feel excluded.

We *respect* powerful men—they know how to take charge. We *resent* powerful men—they're controlling and domineering.

What are we to do? Can't live *with* 'em . . . can't send 'em back to Pluto!

■ ■ ■

A woman's rule of thumb:
If it has tires or testicles,
you're going to have trouble with it.
    —*Women's rest room, Dick's Last Resort, Dallas, Texas*

If they can put a man on the moon, why can't they put all of them there?
    —*anonymous*

If the world were a logical place, men would ride sidesaddle.
    —*Rita Mae Brown*

16

Macho does not prove mucho.

—*Zsa Zsa Gabor*

I like men to behave like men—strong and childish.

—*Françoise Sagan*

Boys will be boys, but girls will be women.

—*Anonymous*

Behind every successful man is a surprised woman.

—*Maryon Pearson*

Women who aspire to be as good as men lack ambition.

—*Anonymous*

Men are taught to apologize for their weaknesses, women for their strengths.

—*Lois Wyse*

If women are supposed to be less rational and more emotional at the beginning of our menstrual cycle, when the female hormone is at its lowest level, then why isn't it logical to say that, in those few days, women behave the most like the way men behave all month long?

—*Gloria Steinem*

When a woman behaves like a man, why doesn't she behave like a nice man?

—*Dame Edith Evans*

The cock may crow, but it's the hen that lays the eggs.

—*Margaret Thatcher*

A man's got to do what a man's got to do. A woman must do what he can't.

—*Rhonda Hansome*

If **high heels** were so *wonderful,* **men** would be **WEARING** them.

—*Sue Grafton*

Men are nicotine soaked, beer besmirched, whiskey greased, red-eyed devils.

—*Carry Nation*

Men are creatures with eight hands.

—*Jayne Mansfield*

Men know they are sexual exiles. They wander the earth seeking satisfaction, craving and despising, never content. There is nothing in that anguished motion for women to envy.

—*Camille Paglia*

Men aren't the way they are because they want to drive women crazy; they've been trained to be that way for thousands of years. And that training makes it very difficult for men to be intimate.

—*Barbara De Angelis*

Men weren't really the enemy—they were fellow victims suffering from an outmoded masculine mystique that made them feel unnecessarily inadequate when there were no bears to kill.

—*Betty Friedan*

If it wasn't for women, men would still be hanging from trees.

—*Marilyn Peterson*

It's a man's world, and you men can have it.
—*Katherine Anne Porter*

Whether women are better than men I cannot say—but I can say they are certainly no worse.
—*Golda Meir*

I love the male body; it's better designed than the male mind.

—Andrea Newman

A woman's body is a work of art. A man's body is utilitarian. It's for gettin' around. It's like a Jeep.

—Elaine, Seinfeld
(on why men shouldn't walk around naked)

I require three things in a man: He must be handsome, ruthless, and stupid.

—Dorothy Parker

A man has only one escape from his old self: to see a different self in the mirror of some woman's eyes.

—Clare Boothe Luce

WORK LIFE
The Rat Race

■ ■ ■

It's no accident that business life is referred to by such terms as "the rat race," "the jungle," and "a dog-eat-dog world." Business best-sellers tell us how to "swim with the sharks" or how to be smart mice in our maze when someone "moves our cheese." We can join the "flight of the buffalo" and participate when "elephants learn to dance." We can even read about how to be a "peacock in the land of penguins." It seems you have to be some kind of *animal* to thrive in today's world of work! Or, as Lily Tomlin quipped, "The problem with the rat race is that, even if you win, you're still a rat."

It's no wonder that three-fourths of all new businesses started these days are started by women! Who needs to hang around in organizations playing a game we can't possibly win? Those headaches we suffer from are caused by banging our heads against the glass ceiling all day!

As you climb the ladder of success,
don't let the boys look up your dress!

—*Jenifer Bunis*

No matter how cynical you get, it is impossible
to keep up.

—*Lily Tomlin*

Cynicism is an unpleasant way of saying the
truth.

—*Lillian Hellman*

I began wearing hats as a young lawyer because
it helped me to establish my professional
identity. Before that, whenever I was at a
meeting, someone would ask me to get the
coffee—they assumed I was a secretary.

—*Bella Abzug*

If I had learned to type, I never would have made brigadier general.

—*Elizabeth P. Hoisington*

But once we got far enough along to see that we could achieve male status and power, we recoiled at the idea of doing it on male terms. Why be rats on a treadmill, butting heads constantly, drinking too much, having heart attacks, and falling into affairs with office playthings?

—*Maureen Dowd*

There are very few jobs that actually require a penis or vagina. All other jobs should be open to everybody.

—*Flo Kennedy*

A **woman** has to be **TWICE** as good as a **man** to go **HALF** as far.

—*Fannie Hurst*

After years of banging heads against the glass ceiling, huge numbers of women are realizing that learning how to dress, getting the right degrees, and struggling to fit in are essentially fruitless exercises. Of a certain age and self-awareness, women who are weary of trying to adapt to environments in which they are not welcome are leaving to create companies that fit them.

—*Joline Godfrey*

Women must understand that it's not another woman who is the enemy, but the power structure that sets it up for very few women to get jobs and makes them fight each other for the few goodies that are thrown their way. We don't tend to see structural or institutional problems. We focus on the other person. We can't.

—*Michelle Faludi*

There is nothing to be gained from women wasting their time trying to change organizations that don't get it now and never will.

—*Kathleen Kelley Reardon*

Women are often shut out at meetings. After a while they pull back. They need to learn how to interject themselves into the action. In many organizations, men do a lot of positioning and posturing. That's how it looks to women. For women, it's like entering a boxing ring. It's a gamesmanship of sorts. When I complained about this to one of my male peers, he told me, "It's all part of keeping each other sharp." There are unwritten rules of the road. The people who survive are the ones who learn them and can work with them.

—*Shirley Peterson*

Sexual static is like snow on the television set or noise on the radio—it causes interference with messages being communicated. In the work-place, . . . both men and women experience sexual static. It causes frustration for women and discomfort for men. Women are frustrated because they feel the static could be minimized if men understood gender differences. Men just want the static to go away.

—*Judy Rosener*

If it's true that men today value their lives outside of work as much as women do—and research proves it is—then they have to join women's fight to reconstruct the way we work and create a new, broader definition of success.

—*Elizabeth Perle*

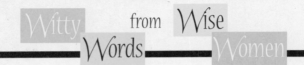

You have to do what you love to do, not get stuck in that comfort zone of a regular job. Life is not a dress rehearsal. This is it.

—Lucinda Basset

If there is a God and an afterlife, I'll have the opportunity to do the same work up there.

—Christie Hefner

Sexual harassment at work—is it a problem for the self-employed?

—Victoria Wood

SUCCESS

What Do Women Really Want?

■ ■ ■

How do you spell *success*? Here's how I spell it:

> **S**elf-acceptance and self-love
> **U**nlimited happiness and fulfillment
> **C**ontribution and service to others
> **C**ommitment to relationships
> **E**nergy and Enthusiasm for life
> **S**elf-determination
> **S**piritual growth and Serenity

It's so easy to get seduced into believing other people's definitions of success: job promotions, financial gain, fame, recognition, status, competitive achievement, trophies, awards, power, et cetera. Not that those things

aren't important and good—they are. But they are not the *only* things. Success is also about relationships, creativity and self-expression, learning and growing, and making a difference in the world.

Success is as much about who you're *being* as what you're *doing*.

Success is not a destination—it's the journey.

■ ■ ■

Women want men, careers, money, children, friends, luxury, comfort, independence, freedom, respect, love, and a three-dollar panty hose that won't run.

—*Phyllis Diller*

They say getting thin is the best revenge. Success is much better.

—*Oprah Winfrey*

32

Success

Behind every successful woman . . . is a basket of dirty laundry.

—Sally Forth

Instead of thinking about where you are, think about where you want to be. It takes twenty years of hard work to become an overnight success.

—Diana Rankin

Without a goal to work toward, we will not get there.

—Natasha Josefowitz

Your goal should be out of reach but not out of sight.

—Anita DeFrantz

Goals are dreams with deadlines.

—Diana Scharf Hunt

The formula for success is simple: practice and concentration, then more practice and more concentration.

—*Babe Didrikson Zaharias*

We can do anything we want to do if we stick with it long enough.

—*Helen Keller*

Success is not a doorway, it's a staircase.

—*Dottie Walters*

You've got to take the initiative and play your game. In a decisive set, confidence is the difference.

—*Chris Evert*

If you don't act as if your name were on the door, it never will be.

—*Patricia Fripp*

To follow, without halt, one aim: There's the secret of success.

—Anna Pavlova

Good enough never is.

—Debbi Fields

Please know that I am quite aware of the hazards. I want to do it because I want to do it. Women must try to do things as men have tried. When they fail, their failure must be but a challenge to others.

—Amelia Earhart (written to her husband before her attempted flight across the Pacific)

Always be smarter than the people who hire you.
—Lena Horne

No one can arrive from being talented alone. God gives talent; work transforms talent into genius.
—Anna Pavlova

If you think you can, you're right.
And if you think you can't, you're right.

—*Mary Kay Ash*

Success is often achieved by those who don't
know that failure is inevitable.

—*Coco Chanel*

Set your goals high and don't let anybody tell
you no.

—*Muriel Siebert*

I didn't get here by dreaming about it or
thinking about it—I got here by doing it.

—*Estée Lauder*

Think big, start small.

—*Patricia Fripp*

Bite off **MORE**

than you *can* chew,

then ***chew*** it.

—*Ella Williams*

My mother drew a distinction between achievement and success. She said that achievement is the knowledge that you have studied and worked hard and done the best that is in you. Success is being praised by others. That is nice but not as important or satisfying. Always aim for achievement and forget about success.

—*Helen Hayes*

Where I was born and where and how I have lived is unimportant. It is what I have done with where I have been that should be of interest.

—*Georgia O'Keeffe*

If you believe that success is getting to the top of a particular mountain, all you find when you get there is the possibility of losing what you already had. "There's no there there," Gertrude Stein once famously said. . . . The outcome never appears the way we had planned it and is always out of our control. The process is the joy.

—*Lynda Obst*

I never wanted success if it meant clawing my way over other bodies. I always knew that would make it pretty lonely once I got there.

—*Barbara Grogan*

Fear of success can also be tied in to the idea that success means someone else's loss. Some people are unconsciously guilty because they believe their victories are coming at the expense of another.

—*Joan C. Harvey*

Success can make you go one of two ways. It can make you a prima donna, or it can smooth the edges, take away the insecurities, let the nice things come out.

—*Barbara Walters*

"Today is the first day of the rest of your life" is a bit portentous; I prefer to wake up to five-card-draw poker. Each morning, a new hand; some days, junk; some days, a full house; and every day, the challenge of playing that hand to win.

—*Wendy Reid Crisp*

"How does one become a butterfly?" she asked pensively. "You must want to fly so much that you are willing to give up being a caterpillar."

—*Trina Paulus*

Develop confidence in yourself and act as if you have it until you do.

—*Barbara Krouse*

STRUGGLE AND
DISAPPOINTMENT

Indomitable Spirit

■ ■ ■

$\mathcal{Y}$ears ago I was writing a book on autobiographies and in my research discovered that the life stories that are really interesting and engaging are the ones in which individuals had to overcome obstacles and rise to meet difficult challenges. Problems test our character and our ability. Obstacles challenge us to think creatively and figure out how to go under, over, around, or through them on our way to our goals. When the odds are stacked against us, we often rise to the occasion and surprise people . . . including ourselves!

Many of us learn more from our failures than we do from our successes. Failure can be a valuable teacher. Failure is often the precursor to success, showing us what

we need to learn and where to put our energy if we are to achieve our dreams.

To be sure, struggle, disappointment, and failure are not fun. A girlfriend once told me that "experience is what you get when you don't get what you want." But invariably that experience proves to be a valuable resource.

Successful people will tell you that if you never experience failure, you're not taking enough risks. And many people, when they look back on their lives, will tell you that they don't regret the things they did; they regret the things they *didn't* do.

Living life to the fullest means that sometimes you fall on your face. Or sometimes you give it all you've got and still come up short. But if you haven't struggled and failed, perhaps you're playing it too safe.

We haven't come a long way, we've come a short way. If we hadn't come a short way, no one would be calling us "baby."

—*Elizabeth Janeway*

The hardest years in life are those between ten and seventy.

—*Helen Hayes*
(spoken when she was eighty-two)

If you can keep your head about you when all about you are losing theirs, it's just possible you haven't grasped the situation.

—*Jean Kerr*

The way I see it, if you want the rainbow, you gotta put up with the rain.

—*Dolly Parton*

Just *don't* give up trying
to do what you **REALLY**
WANT to do. Where there is
love and *inspiration*,
I don't think you can go wrong.

—*Ella Fitzgerald*

44

Struggle and Disappointment

Every time I close the door on reality, it comes in through the windows.

—Jennifer Unlimited

In order to have great happiness, you have to have great pain and unhappiness—otherwise how would you know when you're happy?

—Leslie Caron

Life is easier to take than you'd think; all that is necessary is to accept the impossible, do without the indispensable, and bear the intolerable.

—Kathleen Norris

Nothing, I am sure, calls forth the faculties so much as being obliged to struggle with the world.

—Mary Wollstonecraft

There are hazards in everything one does; but there are greater hazards in doing nothing.
—*Shirley Williams*

Only through trial and suffering is the soul strengthened.
—*Helen Keller*

A chicken doesn't stop scratching just because worms are scarce.
—*Anonymous*

We don't know who we are until we see what we can do.
—*Martha Grimes*

My passions were all gathered together like fingers that made a fist. Drive is considered aggression today; I knew it then as purpose.
—*Bette Davis*

Courage is fear that has said its prayers.
—*Dorothy Bernard*

The only failure one should fear is not hugging to the purpose they see as best.
—*George Eliot*

If you are never scared, embarrassed, or hurt, it means you never take chances.
—*Julia Soul*

Getting ahead in a difficult profession requires avid faith in yourself. You must be able to sustain yourself against staggering blows. There is no code of conduct to help beginners. That is why some people with mediocre talent, but with great inner drive, go much further than people with vastly superior talent.
—*Sophia Loren*

It is better to be boldly decisive and risk being wrong than to agonize at length and be right too late.

—*Marilyn Moats Kennedy*

Mistakes are the usual bridge between inexperience and wisdom.

—*Phyllis Theroux*

When I lose a match, I know that I lose on the court and not in life.

—*Gabriela Sabatini*

I wanted to be scared again. . . . I wanted to feel unsure again. That's the only way I learn, the only way I feel challenged.

—*Connie Chung*

To be tested is good. The challenged life may be the best therapist.

—Gail Sheehy

I have become my own version of an optimist. If I can't make it through one door, I'll go through another door—or I'll make a door. Something terrific will come no matter how dark the present.

—Joan Rivers

I am willing to put myself through anything; temporary pain or discomfort means nothing to me as long as I can see that the experience will take me to a new level. I am interested in the unknown, and the only path to the unknown is through breaking barriers, an often painful process.

—Diana Nyad

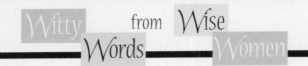
When you have no problems, you're dead.
—*Zelda Werner*

People are like stained-glass windows. They sparkle and shine when the sun is out, but when the darkness sets in, their true beauty is revealed only if there is a light from within.
—*Elisabeth Kübler-Ross*

MONEY

The Best Things in Life Are ... Expensive

■ ■ ■

Germaine Greer once wrote that a woman must have her own money if she is to be truly her own woman. At the time I read this, I didn't understand it, because I had never really been on my own. I had gone directly from my father's house to my husband's house . . . and then back to my father's house when my marriage broke up. I then returned to college, finishing a B.A. degree and pursuing a Ph.D., while living on student loans, scholarships, child support, and financial help from my parents. It wasn't until I was thirty that I left my studies and accepted a full-time job.

I'll never forget how I felt when I got that first real paycheck. There was a rush of pride and self-confidence as I opened the envelope and looked at the check. I suddenly knew what Greer had been writing about. Her words echoed in my mind, and I nodded silently, as if she were

right there in my office and could see me acknowledging her wisdom. Thanks, Germaine, you were right about the money. Now I understand.

■ ■ ■

Money isn't everything . . . but it ranks right up there with oxygen.

—*Rita Davenport*

What I find most disturbing about the 1950s-ification and retrogression of women's lives is that it has seeped into corporate and social culture, where it can do real damage. Otherwise intelligent men, who know women still earn less than men as a rule, say things like: "I'll get the check. You only have girl money."

—*Maureen Dowd*

A fool and her money are soon courted.

—*Helen Rowland*

Does giving birth make me a real woman? No, earning less than a man makes me a real woman.
—*Suzy Berger*

From birth to age eighteen, a girl needs good parents, from eighteen to thirty-five she needs good looks, from thirty-five to fifty-five she needs a good personality, and from fifty-five on she needs cash.
—*Sophie Tucker*

Never marry for money. Ye'll borrow it cheaper.
—*Scottish proverb*

Marrying into money was not a good thing for me.
—*Anna Nicole Smith*

Money does not change men, it only unmasks them.
—*Mme. Marie-Jeanne Riccoboni*

Whether he admits it or not, a man has been brought up to look at money as a sign of his virility, a symbol of his power, a bigger phallic symbol than a Porsche.

—*Victoria Billings*

Money is what you'd get on beautifully without if only other people weren't so crazy about it.

—*Margaret Case Harriman*

The only thing I like about rich people is their money.

—*Lady Nancy Astor*

There are people who have money and people who are rich.

—*Coco Chanel*

All **prosperity** begins
in the MIND and is **dependent**
only upon the **full use** of our
creative imagination.

—*Ruth Ross*

Money is always there, but the pockets change;
it is not in the same pockets after a change,
and that is all there is to say about money.

—Gertrude Stein

The rule is not to talk about money with people
who have much more or much less than you.

—Katharine Whitehorn

People think that being famous is just about
having your picture taken all the time and
being rich, rich, rich, and you know what? . . .
They're absolutely right.

—Madonna

The most beautiful words in the English
language are "Check enclosed."

—Dorothy Parker

Having money is rather like being a blonde.
It is more fun but not vital.

—*Mary Quant*

I don't want to make money. I just want to be
wonderful.

—*Marilyn Monroe*

I've been rich and I've been poor. Rich is better.
—*Sophie Tucker*

Pennies do not come from heaven—they have to
be earned here on earth.

—*Margaret Thatcher*

If you want greater prosperity in your life,
start forming a vacuum to receive it.

—*Catherine Ponder*

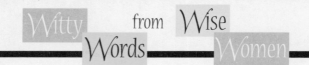

Wealth is the product of man's capacity to think.
—*Ayn Rand*

'Tis a sort of duty to be rich, that it may be in one's power to do good, riches being another word for power.

—*Lady Mary Wortley Montagu*

People make a mistake thinking they are going to be in paradise if they have money.
—*Mahalia Jackson*

Be not too anxious to get money—for nothing worth having can be purchased.

—*Mary Wollstonecraft*

EMPOWERMENT

Can We Have It All?

■ ■ ■

There is an interesting correlation between women's business success and their marital status. If you look at male executives, 95 percent of them are married. If you look at female executives, 80 to 90 percent of them are unmarried. What does that tell us? It tells us that for a man, having a wife means having a support system, someone to provide domestic nurturance while he climbs the corporate ladder. For a woman, having a husband means one more demand on her time, one more person she has to take care of.

Male executives often lament that they have sacrificed time with their families in order to focus on becoming successful leaders. But many women executives sacrifice more than *time*, they sacrifice the possibility of ever *having* a family.

Can we have it all? Well, maybe . . . just not all at once.

Power can be taken, but not given. The process of the taking is empowerment in itself.

—*Gloria Steinem*

"I can support myself," we say proudly, and then we go to support groups, long for supportive husbands, wonder why women aren't supporting other women, demand more support from our institutions, and wear support hose. So where is it written we have to be consistent? . . . We *can* support ourselves, and we want to—except when we don't want to.

—*Wendy Reid Crisp*

Scratch most feminists, and underneath there is a woman who longs to be a sex object. The difference is, that is not *all* she longs to be.

—*Betty Rollin*

Powerful men often succeed through the help of their wives.
Powerful women only succeed in spite of their husbands.

—*Linda Lee-Potter*

If school results were the key to power, girls would be running the world.

—*Sarah Boseley*

You know what real power is? Real power is when you are doing exactly what you are supposed to be doing the best it can be done. Authentic power. There's a surge, there's a kind of energy field that says, "I'm in my groove. I'm in my groove." And nobody has to tell you, "You go, girl," because, you know, you're already gone.

—*Oprah Winfrey*

The things that are important—such as courage, integrity, luck, and determination—those things are not distributed on your chromosomes.

—*Rhonda Cornum*

Sexiness is no longer defined just as whether [women] are desirable, but also as what [women] desire. The more liberated women become—economically, politically, and personally—the more erotic we are. Freedom is a lot sexier than dependency.

—*Naomi Wolf*

I think that women making no apology for being women is very refreshing.

—*Drew Barrymore*

Empowerment

Above all other prohibitions, what has been forbidden to women is anger, together with the open admission of the desire for power and control over one's own life.

—*Carolyn Heilbrun*

I became a feminist as an alternative to becoming a masochist.

—*Sally Kempton*

A woman reading *Playboy* feels a little like a Jew reading a Nazi manual.

—*Gloria Steinem*

People call me a feminist whenever I express sentiments that differentiate me from a doormat or a prostitute.

—*Rebecca West*

As a woman
I have no **COUNTRY.**
As a woman *my country*
is the **whole world**.

—*Virginia Woolf*

I'm tough, ambitious, and I know exactly what I want. If that makes me a bitch, okay.

—*Madonna*

The point of women's liberation is not to stand at the door of the male world, beating our fists, and crying, "Let me in, damn you, let me in!" The point is to walk away from the world and concentrate on creating a new woman.

—*Vivian Gornick*

If you want to see your daughter succeed, don't just teach her to add and subtract, teach her to deduct.

—*Joan G. Rosenberg*

For what is done or learned by one class of women becomes, by virtue of their common womanhood, the property of all women.

—*Elizabeth Blackwell*

Women's liberation now means being liberated from stereotypes about what women want.

—*Maureen Dowd*

Women typically approach adulthood with the understanding that the care and empowerment of others is central to their life's work. Through listening and responding, they draw out the voices and minds of those they help to raise up. In the process, they often come to hear, value, and strengthen their own voices and minds as well.

—*Mary Field Belenky, Blythe McVicker Clinchy, Nancy Rule Goldberger, and Jill Mattuck Tarule*

I believe it is incredibly important for women to support other women so that in time success and achievement are not remarkable by gender.

—*Brenda Dean*

Empowerment

Ultimately, to get to equality, it's women who will have to lead the way. It's not going to be handed to us. If we've learned one thing, nothing will be gained without a real, intense struggle.

—Eleanor Smeal

The one important thing I have learned over the years is the difference between taking one's work seriously and taking one's self seriously. The first is imperative and the second is disastrous.

—Dame Margot Fonteyn

Efficiency tends to deal with Things.
Effectiveness tends to deal with People.
We *manage* Things, we *lead* People

—Admiral Grace Hopper

I run my company according to feminine principles—principles of caring; making intuitive decisions; not getting hung up on hierarchy or all those dreadfully boring business-school management ideas; having a sense of work as being part of your life, not separate from it; putting your labor where your love is; being responsible to the world in how you use your profits; recognizing the bottom line should stay at the bottom.

—*Anita Roddick*

If they speak in ways expected of women, they are seen as inadequate leaders. If they speak in ways expected of leaders, they are seen as inadequate women. The road to authority is tough for women, and once they get there it's a bed of thorns.

—*Deborah Tannen*

We need to find the courage to say *no* to the things and people that are not serving us if we want to rediscover ourselves and live our lives with authenticity.

—Barbara De Angelis

Women are having to do way too much. They are multitasking, working long hours, and they are still responsible for most of what happens with the family; they are caregivers, best friends, listeners; they are amazing, amazing people.

—Dawn Tarnofsky-Ostroff

We are volcanoes. When we women offer our experience as our truth, as human truth, all the maps change. There are new mountains.

—Ursula K. Le Guin

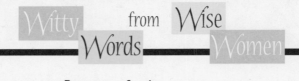
I have **a lot** of things
to prove to *myself*.
One is that *I can*
live FEARLESSLY.

—Oprah Winfrey

70

CREATIVITY AND
SELF-EXPRESSION

Show Your True Colors

■ ■ ■

If you ask a class of kindergartners, "Who here is creative?" a whole roomful of little arms will shoot straight up with a chorus of: "I am, I am!"

If you ask a class of sixth graders, "Who among you is creative?" perhaps a third of the kids will raise their hands.

And if you ask a senior high school class the same question, only a few hands will go up.

What is happening to our creativity? How did we lose faith in our own natural talents to think, create, solve problems, look at things in new ways, use our imaginations, make stuff up from nothing, dream, explore, fantasize, and invent?

As women, we must reclaim our innate creativity. As

mothers, daughters, sisters, friends, lovers, wives, co-workers, and neighbors, we must encourage others to express themselves fully too. Creativity is important in *everything* we do in life, it's not just relegated to spare-time hobbies. It is in our creative work that we fully express who we are. As Toni Morrison points out: "We are traditionally rather proud of ourselves for having slipped creative work in there between the domestic chores and obligations. I'm not sure we deserve such big A-pluses for that."

■ ■ ■

A child's attitude is an artist's attitude.
— *Willa Cather*

I think, at a child's birth, if a mother could ask a fairy godmother to endow it with the most useful gift, that gift would be curiosity.
— *Eleanor Roosevelt*

Creativity and Self-Expression

There is a vitality, a life force, an energy, a quickening that is translated through you into action. And because there is only one of you in all of time, this expression is unique. And if you block it, it will never exist through any other medium and be lost.

It is not your business to determine how good it is nor how valuable nor how it compares with other expressions.

It is your business to . . . keep the channel open. . . . Whether you choose to take an art class, keep a journal, record your dreams, dance your story, or live each day from your own creative source, above all else, keep the channel open!

—Martha Graham

The delights of self-discovery are always available.

—*Gail Sheehy*

Religion and art spring from the same root and are close kin.

—*Willa Cather*

I learned that the real creator was my inner Self. . . . That desire to do something is God inside talking through us.

—*Michele Shea*

Life is raw material. We are artisans. We can sculpt our existence into something beautiful, or debase it into ugliness. It's in our hands.

—*Cathy Better*

We are governed not by armies, but by ideas.

—*Mona Caird*

Creativity and Self-Expression

An original mind is rarely understood.

—*Margaret Fuller*

Creative minds have always been known to survive any kind of bad training.

—*Anna Freud*

Genius is essentially creative; it bears the stamp of the individual who possesses it.

—*Germaine de Staël*

Art is the difference between seeing and just identifying.

—*Jean Mary Norman*

Our senses are indeed our doors and windows on this world, in a very real sense the key to the unlocking of meaning and the wellspring of creativity.

—*Jean Houston*

Creativity is INVENTING,
experimenting, growing,
taking risks, **breaking rules,**
making mistakes,
and *having fun.*

—Mary Lou Cook

The creative urge is the demon that will not accept anything second-rate.

—Agnes de Mille

Every artist makes herself born. You must bring the artist into the world yourself.

—Willa Cather

I believe talent is like electricity. We do not understand electricity. We use it. Electricity makes no judgment. You can plug into it and light up a lamp, keep a heart pump going, light a cathedral, or you can electrocute a person with it. . . . I think talent is like that. I believe every person is born with a talent.

—Maya Angelou

Your passion is waiting for your courage to catch up.

—Marilyn Greist

I have made my world, and it is a much better world than I ever saw outside.

—*Louise Nevelson*

You were once wild here. Don't let them tame you.

—*Isadora Duncan*

If you do things well, do them better. Be daring, be first, be different, be just.

—*Anita Roddick*

When I stand before God at the end of my life, I would hope that I would not have a single bit of talent left and could say: I used everything you gave me.

—*Erma Bombeck*

MAKING A DIFFERENCE
Women's Legacy to the World

■ ■ ■

What do you want to be remembered for when you die? I love to ask people this question. Their answers tell me much about what they're up to in life.

I once had the opportunity to ask Steve Jobs, cofounder of Apple and creator of the Macintosh computer. His answer surprised me. He said, "I want to be remembered as the best father in the whole world." Not what I expected from a living legend—a brilliant man who is a leading pioneer in the technology revolution, and a marketing genius to boot!

If I were to ask *you* the same question, "How do you want to be remembered when you die?" what would your answer be?

You don't have to be world famous to make a difference in the world. Perhaps you are active in your community, or in your church or synagogue. Maybe you are involved in politics. Millions of women make a difference by volunteering in hospitals, hospices, homeless shelters, and social service organizations. Maybe the difference you make is in the arts, with your music, writing, painting, sculpture, or other art form. Perhaps you are one of those angels known as teachers—who make a huge difference by educating our next generation of citizens. And maybe, like Steve Jobs, the difference you are most interested in making is within your own family.

The question is: What will be *your* legacy to the world?

■ ■ ■

Women have got to make the world safe for men since men have made it so darned unsafe for women.

—*Lady Nancy Astor*

You can no more win a war than you can win an earthquake. As a woman, I can't go to war, and I refuse to send anyone else.

—*Jeannette Rankin*

As world events reflect, we remain far from mastering the art of human relations. We have invented no technology that will guide us to the destinations that matter most.

After two world wars, the Holocaust, multiple genocides, and countless conflicts, we must ask how long it will be before we are able to rise above the national, racial, and gender distinctions that divide us, and embrace the common humanity that binds us.

The answer depends not on the stars or some mysterious forces of history; it depends on the choices that you and I and all of us make.

—*Madeleine Albright*

Although the connections are not always obvious, personal change is inseparable from social and political change.

—Harriet Lerner

If one is lucky, a solitary fantasy can totally transform one million realities.

—Maya Angelou

I am in the world to change the world.

—Muriel Rukeyser

If we have the courage and tenacity of our forebears, who stood firmly like a rock against the lash of slavery, we shall find a way to do for our day what they did for theirs.

—Mary McLeod Bethune

I think the day of selfishness is over; the day of really working together has come, and we must learn to work together, all of us, regardless of race or creed or color.

—Eleanor Roosevelt

A small group of committed people can make a difference and change the world.

—Margaret Mead

Idealists . . . foolish enough to throw caution to the winds . . . have advanced mankind and enriched the world.

—Emma Goldman

I want to work for a company that contributes to and is part of the community. I want something not just to invest in. I want something to believe in.

—Anita Roddick

True happiness is not attained through self-gratification, but through fidelity to a worthy cause.

—Helen Keller

Our own success, to be real, must contribute to the success of others.

—Eleanor Roosevelt

My grandfather once told me that there are two kinds of people: those who do the work and those who take the credit. He told me to try to be in the first group; there is much less competition.

—Indira Gandhi

A handful of pine seed will cover mountains with the green majesty of forests. I too will set my face to the wind and throw my handful of seed on high.

—Fiona Macleod

Making a Difference

You have not lived a perfect day . . . unless you have done something for someone who will never be able to repay you.

—*Ruth Smeltzer*

Service is the rent we pay for the privilege of living on this earth.

—*Shirley Chisholm*

One's life has value so long as one attributes value to the life of others, by means of love, friendship, indignation, and compassion.

—*Simone de Beauvoir*

Some people go through life trying to find out what the world holds for them only to find out too late that it's what they bring to the world that really counts.

—*Anne of Green Gables*

You cannot hope to build a better world without improving the individuals. To that end, each of us must work for our own improvement and, at the same time, share a general responsibility for all humanity, our particular duty being to aid those to whom we think we can be most useful.

—Madame Marie Curie

Alone we can do so little; together we can do so much.

—Helen Keller

Life is an exciting business, and most exciting when lived for others.
I am a pencil in the hand of God.

—Mother Teresa of Calcutta

If I can stop one heart from breaking, I shall not live in vain.

—Emily Dickinson

LOVE AND MARRIAGE
Living Happily Ever After?

■ ■ ■

I've often felt that I grew up kind of schizophrenic—living in the tension between two polar opposites. I was a child in the '50s, a time of peaceable prosperity and industrious optimism. But I came of age in the '60s, a decade of rambunctious rebellion and a hybrid cynicism-idealism. I can't decide if I should live in "The World According to Ozzie and Harriet" or "The World According to Betty Friedan and Gloria Steinem."

This schizophrenia shows up most vividly in my love life. In the '50s I assumed I would grow up, go to college, get a job for a little while, get married, and raise a family—in that order. My stay-at-home mom fit the role models I saw on TV and in the community where we lived. But the '60s gave me a whole new set of possibilities for my love life:

free love, the sexual revolution, and "if you can't be with the one you love, love the one you're with."

Today, I guess I've adopted the Burger King motto: "Have it your way." The eclectic values of a diverse, pluralistic society offer a variety of models for love, with or without marriage. Love and marriage is now a multiple-choice question:

- lifelong marriage to one partner
- serial monogamy
- living together unmarried
- same-sex partnership
- single, looking for Mr. Right
- single, will settle for Mr. Right Now
- single, not interested, thank you very much

■ ■ ■

Love is a fire. But whether it is going to warm your hearth or burn down your house, you can never tell.

—*Joan Crawford*

If it is your time, love will track you down like a cruise missile.

—Lynda Barry

You can't put a price tag on love, but you can on all its accessories.

—Melanie Clark

Infatuation is when you think he's as sexy as Robert Redford, as smart as Henry Kissinger, as noble as Ralph Nader, as funny as Woody Allen, and as athletic as Jimmy Connors. Love is when you realize that he's as sexy as Woody Allen, as smart as Jimmy Connors, as funny as Ralph Nader, as athletic as Henry Kissinger, and nothing like Robert Redford—but you love him anyway.

— Judith Viorst

We **had** a lot in common.
I *loved him* and
he loved **him**.

—Shelley Winters

Love and Marriage

Do you want me to tell you something really subversive? Love is everything it's cracked up to be. That's why people are so cynical about it. It really is worth fighting for, being brave for, risking everything for. And the trouble is, if you don't risk anything, you risk even more.

—*Erica Jong*

The pain of love is the pain of being alive. It is a perpetual wound.

—*Maureen Duffy*

The sweetest joy, the wildest woe is love.

—*Pearl Bailey*

There is only one happiness in life—to love and to be loved.

—*George Sand*

The truth is that there is only one terminal dignity—love. And the story of a love is not important—what is important is that one is capable of love. It is perhaps the only glimpse we are permitted of eternity.

—*Helen Hayes*

In real love, you want the other person's good. In romantic love, you want the other person.

—*Margaret Anderson*

"Love" is the same as "like" except you feel sexier.

—*Judith Viorst*

My last stab at romantic love ran out at the exact same time as his bottle of hair spray in my bathroom.

—*Roberta Freeman*

It's not the men in my life that count, it's the life in my men.

—*Mae West*

Women might be able to fake orgasms. But men can fake entire relationships.

—*Sharon Stone*

Love is like the measles, all the worse when it comes late.

—*Mary Roberts Rinehart*

Marriage is a great institution, but I'm not ready for an institution, yet.

—*Mae West*

Men who have a pierced ear are better prepared for marriage—they've experienced pain and bought jewelry.

—*Rita Rudner*

A man in love is incomplete until he is married.
Then he's finished.

—*Zsa Zsa Gabor*

I married beneath me. All women do.

—*Lady Nancy Astor*

Marriage is a bargain. And somebody has to
get the worst of a bargain.

—*Helen Rowland*

There is so little difference between husbands,
you might as well keep the first.

—*Adele Rogers St. Johns*

A liberated woman is one who has sex before
marriage and a job after.

—*Gloria Steinem*

Love and Marriage

You see a lot of smart guys with dumb women, but you hardly ever see a smart woman with a dumb guy.

—*Erica Jong*

The only thing a man's good *for,* he's not very good *at.*

—*Peg Bundy,* Married . . . with Children

Sometimes I wonder if men and women really suit each other. Perhaps they should live next door and just visit now and then.

—*Katharine Hepburn*

When he is late for dinner, I know he must be either having an affair or lying dead in the street. I always hope it's the street.

—*Judith Viorst*

I go for two kinds of men. The kind with muscles, and the kind without.

—*Mae West*

Love is blind—marriage is the eye-opener.

—*Pauline Thomason*

Marrying a man is like buying something you've been admiring for a long time in a shop window. You may love it when you get it home, but it doesn't always go with everything else in the house.

—*Jean Kerr*

Some women can be fooled all of the time, and all women can be fooled some of the time, but the same woman can't be fooled by the same man in the same way more than half of the time.

—*Helen Rowland*

Husbands are awkward things to deal with; even keeping them in hot water will not make them tender.

—*Mary Buckley*

Agree with everything he says, and then do what you want anyway.

—*Grandma Helen*

To fall in love is easy, even to remain in it is not difficult; our human loneliness is cause enough. But is a hard quest worth making to find a comrade through whose steady presence one becomes steadily the person one desires to be?

—*Anna Strong*

The easiest kind of relationship is with ten thousand people, the hardest is with one.

—*Joan Baez*

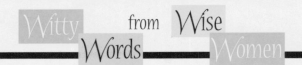

The ultimate test of a relationship is to disagree but to hold hands.

—*Alexandra Penney*

No one worth possessing can be quite possessed.

—*Sara Teasdale*

MOTHERHOOD AND FAMILY

Kids, Kith, and Kin

■ ■ ■

I hear people talking a lot lately about "family values," but what does *family* mean? Does *family* mean a mom, dad, and 2.2 kids in a house with a white picket fence and a dog in the yard? Does *family* mean a big, rollicking extended family of cousins, aunts and uncles, grandparents, with some friends thrown into the mix? If I'm a single mother with one child and two cats, does that qualify us as a *family*?

What if I feel more loved by my circle of close friends than I do by my biological family? Who do I consider my "real" family? Can I build my own family of choice?

We have mixed feelings about our families, and about mothers in particular. We have Barbara Bush and Rose Kennedy as political mothers; Lucille Ball and Donna Reed as TV mothers; Joan Crawford and Judy Garland as movie mothers; Cher and Madonna as musical mothers; Ruth

Handler as the mother of the Barbie doll and Jill Barad as Barbie's beautiful but bad former stepmother; Golda Meir and Indira Gandhi as the mothers of countries; and spiritual mothers, like Mother Teresa and the Virgin of Guadalupe. And we even have surrogate mothers, Oprah and Martha Stewart. Oprah is the mother we wish we had because she is so imperfectly human, while Martha is the mother that many of us love to hate because she is far too perfect.

Being a mother carries a great deal of significance. Mothers are either sanctified or vilified. Mothers are rarely regarded as female humans who have the daunting responsibility of the most important job on the planet—birthing and raising the next generation of humans. We have such mixed feelings about our own mothers, yet here we are, trying to overcome the mothering we received in order to be better mothers to our own kids. And, finally, the ultimate motherhood experience: looking in the mirror one morning only to discover that you're turning into your mother.

So . . . now, who's ready to go home for the holidays?

Motherhood and Family

I want to have children, but my friends scare me. One of my friends told me she was in labor for thirty-six hours. I don't even want to do anything that feels good for thirty-six hours.

—*Rita Rudner*

It's not easy being a mother. If it were easy, fathers would do it.

—*Dorothy,* The Golden Girls

The phrase "working mother" is redundant.

—*Jane Sellman*

Motherhood and homemaking are honorable choices for any woman, provided it is the woman herself who makes those decisions.

—*Molly Yard*

My mother is a woman who speaks with her life as well as her tongue.

—*Kesaya E. Noda*

If help and salvation are to come, they can only come from the children, for the children are the makers of men.

—*Maria Montessori*

Children are apt to live up to what you believe of them.

—*Lady Bird Johnson*

Children have more need of models than of critics.

—*Carolyn Coats*

The word *no* carries a lot more meaning when spoken by a parent who also knows how to say *yes*.

—*Joyce Maynard*

How simple a thing it seems to me that, to know ourselves as we are, we must know our mothers' names.

—*Alice Walker*

Having a **baby** gives you
a SENSE of what's
really important.
You still *work like hell,*
but it's all in PERSPECTIVE.

—Nancy Badore

If that '50s style of mothering has vanished, so too has the '70s belief that to have a life of work and accomplishment, a woman has to pass up motherhood. . . . The debate whether a woman can be both a mother and be employed is moot. The question of how to do both is very much alive.

—*Caryl Rivers and Rosalind C. Barnett*

Nobody has ever before asked the nuclear family to live all by itself in a box the way we do. With no relatives, no support, we've put it in an impossible situation.

—*Margaret Mead*

Call it a clan, call it a network, call it a tribe, call it a family: Whatever you call it, whoever you are, you need one.

—*Jane Howard*

Where thou art, that is home.

—*Emily Dickinson*

"Home" is any four walls that enclose the right person.

—*Helen Rowland*

The woman is the home. That's where she used to be, and that's where she still is. You might ask me, What if a man tries to be part of the home—will the woman let him? I answer yes. Because then he becomes one of the children.

—*Marguerite Duras*

An ounce of mother is worth a pound of clergy.

—*Spanish proverb*

Biological possibility and desire are not the same as biological need. Women have child-bearing equipment. For them to choose not to use the equipment is no more blocking what is instinctive than it is for a man who, muscles or no, chooses not to be a weight lifter.

—*Betty Rollin*

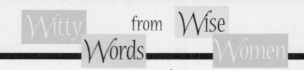
Total commitment to family and total commitment to career is possible, but fatiguing.

—*Muriel Fox*

You need not feel guilty about not being able to keep your life perfectly balanced. Juggling everything is too difficult. All you really need to do is catch it before it hits the floor!

—*Carol Bartz*

Parents are often so busy with the physical rearing of children that they miss the glory of parenthood, just as the grandeur of the trees is lost when raking leaves.

—*Marcelene Cox*

Most American children suffer too much mother and too little father.

—*Gloria Steinem*

INSPIRATION
Food for Our Souls

■ ■ ■

Where do we look for inspiration? Dr. Rachel Naomi Remen writes:

> When we haven't the time to listen to each
> other's stories we seek out experts to teach us
> how to live. The less time we spend together at
> the kitchen table, the more how-to books appear
> in the stores and on our bookshelves. . . .
> Because we have stopped listening to each other,
> we may even have forgotten how to listen,
> stopped learning how to recognize meaning.

We don't need experts with Ph.D.'s to tell us how to live wonderful lives. We need only look to other women. Our world abounds with inspiring women—women who overcome seemingly impossible difficulties, women who follow their dreams into uncharted territory, women who rise to incredible heights of achievement and success. Inspiring women teach us how to find spiritual fulfillment, creative expression, and deep satisfaction in life.

Who feeds our souls with spiritual food? Other women do, that's who.

■ ■ ■

Where there is a woman there is magic.

—Ntozake Shange

It is not easy to find happiness in ourselves, and it is not possible to find it elsewhere.

—Agnes Repplier

We don't see things as they are, we see things as *we* are.

—Anaïs Nin

A woman at peace has stopped looking for someone to blame.

—*Barbara Jenkins*

Character—the willingness to accept responsibility for one's own life—is the source from which self-respect springs.

—*Joan Didion*

Love is the great miracle cure. Loving ourselves works miracles in our lives.

—*Louise L. Hay*

Life is what we make it; always has been, always will be.

—*Grandma Moses*

Never fear shadows. They simply mean there's a light shining somewhere nearby.

—*Ruth E. Renkel*

Feel the fear and do it anyway.

— Susan Jeffers

Don't be afraid your life will end; be afraid it will never begin.

— Grace Hansen

Without faith, nothing is possible. With faith, nothing is impossible.

— Mary McLeod Bethune

Women hold up half the sky.

— Chinese proverb

Seek not good from without: Seek it within yourselves, or you will never find it.

— Bertha von Suttner

Always be a first-rate version of yourself, instead of a second-rate version of somebody else.

— Judy Garland

The **future** belongs to those
who *believe* in the
beauty of their **dreams**.

—*Eleanor Roosevelt*

The very least you can do in your life is to figure out what you hope for. And the most you can do is live inside that hope. Not admire it from a distance but live right in it, under its roof.

—*Barbara Kingsolver*

The Golden Rule works for men as written, but for women it should go the other way around. We need to do unto ourselves as we do unto others.

—*Gloria Steinem*

Why do they always teach us that it's easy and evil to do what we want and that we need discipline to restrain ourselves? It's the hardest thing in the world to do what we want, and it takes the greatest kind of courage.

—*Ayn Rand*

All things are possible until they are proved impossible—and even the impossible may only be so, as of now.

—*Pearl S. Buck*

I think you have to take charge of your own life and understand that you're either going to live somebody else's dream or live your own dream.

—*Wilma Mankiller*

Character is what you know you are, not what others think you have.

—*Marva Collins*

Life was meant to be lived, and curiosity must be kept alive. One must never, for whatever reason, turn her back on life.

—*Eleanor Roosevelt*

Life loves the liver of it.

—*Maya Angelou*

When you were born, you cried and the world rejoiced. Live your life in such a manner that when you die, the world cries and you rejoice.

—*Indian mother's lullaby*

"Yes" is contagious on a subliminal level. It affects everything you do.

—*SARK*

Desire, ask, believe, receive.

—*Stella Terrill Mann*

You need to claim the events of your life to make yourself yours.

—*Anne Wilson Schaef*

Since you are like no other being ever created since the beginning of time, you are incomparable.
—*Brenda Ueland*

Life itself is the proper binge.
—*Julia Child*

To the ancient Chinese curse "May you live in interesting times," we can add the feminist hex "May you live with unlimited options," and when they present themselves, just say yes. Losing your mind is a small price to pay for an interesting life.
—*Wendy Reid Crisp*

If everyone lit their own candle, the whole world would be lit.
—*Mary Moskovitz*

Remember: "Impossible" means "I'm possible."
—*SARK*

Index

About the Author

B. J. Gallagher Hateley lives in Los Angeles and is one of the few people who really loves it there. She makes her living with words—writing books, teaching seminars, and giving keynote speeches at conferences. Every woman's dream—getting paid to talk!

She lives in a small hilltop house with a beautiful view of the city and seven cats for company. Her son, Michael Hateley, is a rock musician (isn't every young man in L.A.?) who wears black and drives an old Cadillac hearse. B. J. never should have taken him to see the movie *Harold and Maude* when he was little.

B. J. is the coauthor of numerous books, including the best-selling *A Peacock in the Land of Penguins*. Her two newest books are *What Would Buddha Do at Work?* and *Is It Always Right to Be Right?*

B. J. is available to speak to women's groups, conferences, and businesses. You can contact her at (323) 227-6205 or www.bjgallagher.com.